SILLY EGGS: a recipe book

Author: Marlene Miles

Freshwater Press

Freshwaterpress9@gmail.com

ISBN: 978-1-971933-46-7

Paperback Version

DEDICATION:

This book is dedicated to the real ones:
The folks who wake up at 3:17 a.m. needing pickles and marshmallows.
The ones who have cried over a missing hot sauce bottle.
The ones currently carrying a baby, a bloat, or a beautifully weird desire to eat cheddar and chocolate on the same plate.

Welcome home. This book was basically made for you.

WARNING:

In whatever state you create or intake these deviled eggs, be careful of textures and consistencies. Especially with small and crushed things be careful when giving to very small children or even older people or adults in various "states" of awareness to avoid choking.

This book is intended for creative purpose, for fun and enjoyment under normal circumstances and in normal states of awareness and sobriety.

Keep small objects away from children, especially unsupervised children.

Table of Contents

How to Use This Book Without Crying or Calling Mom 8
The Egg That Saved a Marriage 10
SILLY EGGS (& MAYBE SWEET) 13
Gummy Worm Surprise 15
Animal Safari Cracker Carnival 17
Apple Slice + Caramel Drizzle 19
Bacon Bit Bonanza 21
Banana Slice & Peanut Butter Drizzle 23
Candy Corn Hat Deviled Egg 25
Cereal Marshmallows Only (Lucky Charms Style) 27
Chocolate Chip Hat 29
Cotton Candy Puff 31
Cotton Candy + Pop Rocks 34
Crushed Froot Loops Confetti 36
Crushed Oreo & Cream Cheese Dot 38
Fruit Loop Halo 40
Graham Cracker & Apple Butter Swirl Deviled Egg 42
Gummy Bear Hug 44
Jelly Bean Sparkle Deviled Egg 46

Mini Marshmallows & Pop Rocks 48

Pancake (Mini) with Syrup Dot 50

Peanut Butter & Banana Chip Duo 52

Peep-A-Boo, I See You 53

Candy Hop (Bunny Peeps) 54

Sandy Beach Deviled Egg 56

S'mores Crumble (Graham + Choc + Marshmallow) 58

Sour Patch Kid Sidekick 60

Sprinkle Me Silly (Rainbow Sprinkles) 62

Teddy Graham + Sprinkle 64

Waffle (Mini) Deviled Egg 66

CRUNCHY (& RIDICULOUS). Party Eggs with Award Winning Chaos 67

Mini Bagel Chip & Cream Cheese Dot 69

BBQ Potato Chip Crunch 71

Cool Ranch Doritos Crumble 73

Mini Crouton & Caesar Sprinkle 75

Crushed Cheese Puffs & Pickle Dust 77

Crushed Doritos & Salsa Dot 79

Pretzel Stick Wand 81

Flamin' Hot Cheetos Crumble 83

Mini French Fry & Ketchup Dot 85
Frosted Flake Crown 87
Fruit Snack Frenzy 89
Funyon Onion Ring Loop 91
Potato Sticks "Bird's Nest" 93
Mini Queso Dip & Tortilla Chip Shard 95
Ranch Seasoning & Cheez-It Hat 97
Crushed Takis Tornado 99
OUT THERE (& MAYBE SAVORY) 100
Candy Bacon Crumbles 102
Mini Corn Dog Deviled Egg 104
Cornbread Cube + Hot Sauce 106
Falafel & Cucumber Dot 108
Tiny Ham Cube & Pineapple Sliver 110
Tiny Meatball & Parmesan Sprinkle 112
Pepperoni & Mozzarella (Pizza Egg) 114
Mini Pickle Slice 116
Sausage Link Crown 118
Sloppy Joe Slather 120
Taco Shell & Salsa Dot 122

String Bean Tempura Swords 124
Green Peas (Green Polka Dots) 126
Mini Fried Chicken Nugget Chunk 127
TOTALLY WEIRD (but we love them) 128
Gummy Pizza Slice 130
Ketchup & Mustard Zigzag 132
PB&J Dot Combo 133
Spray Cheese Swirl 136
Nutella Me About It Deviled Egg 138
Banana & Bacon Remix Deviled Egg 140
Mini Cheese Ritz Cracker Cap 142
Rice Krispies Snap-Crackle-Crunch 144
Toasted Mini Marshmallow & Chocolate Chip 146
Crumbled Cookie Dough Bites 148
Tater Tot Top Hat 150
Fried Mac & Cheese Ball 151
Hot Tamales Deviled Eggs 153
Jalapeño Popper Deviled Egg 155
Melt Down in the Middle (Grilled Cheese Deviled Egg) 158
Bugged Out (Celery + PB + Raisins – Ants on a Deviled Egg) 160

Pickle Chip & Ranch Dust Bomb 162
Trail Mix Madness 164
Pastabilities 166
Loaded Nacho Egg (Sour Cream, Jalapeño, Cheese, Chips) 168
Deviled Egg Biscuit Sandwich 169

How to Use This Book Without Crying or Calling Mom

(*Though calling her to brag is fully encouraged.*)

Welcome to **Silly Deviled Eggs** — the cookbook for kids, teens, college students, and grownups who can barely boil water but still want to impress people with something weird and wonderful. This book isn't about precision or perfection. It's about vibes, yolks, and chaos.

Here's how to survive it:

Step 1: Boil Some Eggs.

Yes, for real. If you don't know how, Google it. Or ask literally anyone with a kitchen. If you do know how, congrats — you're now a chef.

Step 2: Make the Basic Deviled Egg Mix.

We've included the classic Southern-style filling (page 3), and we use it for almost every recipe. It's simple: yolks, mayo, mustard, salt, and pepper. No rocket science. Just mash it up.

Step 3: Pick a Topping From This Glorious Egg Circus.

Sweet? Crunchy? Spicy? Totally unhinged? You choose the flavor chaos. We've got over 60 ideas. Some are surprisingly delicious. Some are just… surprising.

Step 4: Assemble With Confidence and No Shame.

Spoon or pipe the filling back into the egg whites. Top it like a legend. Use your hands. Lick the spoon. Decorate with no fear of judgment. This is a safe zone.

Step 5: Serve with Flair.

Host a party. Take a selfie with your egg. Hand it to a friend and say, "I made this and I don't know why." Then watch them eat it anyway.

Pro Tips (a.k.a. Egg Warnings):

- Don't put Pop Rocks or cotton candy on too early unless you want goo.
- Don't microwave your egg with a Cheez-It on top. It gets weird.
- Don't trust anyone who says deviled eggs aren't brunch-worthy.
- Always carry napkins. Some of these eggs are super messy.
- If someone asks for the recipe? Just say, *"It's in the book."*

Wanna do some crazy combinations with deviled eggs? Permission granted. Carry on.

The Egg That Saved a Marriage

She was 7 months pregnant.
He was 100% clueless.

She turned to him in the middle of the night and

whispered:

"I need something. It's sweet... no, salty... it has cheese... and maybe a crunch? I don't know. It's... it's like an egg... but not boring!"

He blinked. He panicked.
"Do you want a sandwich?"
"DO I LOOK LIKE I WANT A SANDWICH?"

There were tears.
There were pickles thrown.
He was on the verge of sleeping in the car.

Then, from the kitchen counter...
She grabbed the book, ***Silly Deviled Eggs***.
She turned to page 23.
She pointed. **Firmly.**

“This. This is it. *The King’s Yolk*. With banana, peanut butter, and egg. THIS IS WHAT I **NEED**.”

He made it.
She devoured it.
She wept softly.
He was forgiven.

That night, a marriage was saved by one egg —
And a very silly cookbook.

Because sometimes, all you need is a deviled egg topped with crushed Doritos and a gummy worm… just to feel seen.

SILLY EGGS (& MAYBE SWEET)

These are the dessert eggs. Yes, they're weird. Yes, they're tasty. Yes, they're silly. And they are first because sometimes we should have desert first.

Gummy Worm Surprise

Gummy Worm Surprise

The Early Bird Gets the Worm

Ingredients:

6 hard-boiled eggs, peeled

3 tbsp mayonnaise

1 tsp yellow mustard

1/2 tsp pickle juice (optional)

Salt & pepper, to taste

6 mini gummy worms (or regular ones cut in half)

Instructions:

Prep the Filling:
Slice eggs in half, scoop out yolks, and mash with mayo, mustard, pickle juice, salt, and pepper.

Fill the Eggs:
Spoon or pipe the yolk mixture back into the egg whites.

Add the Gummy Worm:
Press a mini gummy worm gently into the yolk filling so it looks like it's crawling out of the egg.
Optional: Twist or bend the worm for max wiggle effect.

Serve with Giggles:
Perfect for Halloween, pranks, or confusing brunch guests.

Animal Safari Cracker Carnival

Animal Safari Cracker Carnival

A deviled egg topped with a classic animal cracker (like an elephant or giraffe) pressed into the creamy yolk filling

Ingredients:

- 6 hard-boiled eggs, peeled
- 3 tbsp mayonnaise, 1 tsp yellow mustard
- 1/2 tsp honey (optional, for sweetness)
- Salt & pepper, to taste
- 6 animal crackers (any classic animal shape)
- Optional: edible confetti sprinkles or cookie crumbs

Instructions:

1. **Make the Filling:**
   Slice eggs, remove yolks, and mash with mayo, mustard, honey, salt, and pepper until creamy.
2. **Fill with Fun:**
   Spoon or pipe the yolk mixture into the egg whites.
3. **Top with Animal Cracker:**
   Press one animal cracker upright into each deviled egg like it's on a carnival ride.
   Optional: sprinkle with edible confetti or cookie crumbs for full "carnival chaos" look.
4. **Serve Wild & Free:**
   Best served on a colorful snack tray at a party where no one's taking life too seriously.

Apple Slice + Caramel Drizzle

Apple Slice + Caramel Drizzle

Fall festival flavor. Zero adult supervision. A deviled egg topped with a thin apple slice and elegant caramel sauce.

Ingredients:

- 6 hard-boiled eggs, peeled
- 3 tbsp mayonnaise, 1 tsp yellow mustard, 1 tsp apple cider vinegar (for tang)
- Salt & pepper, to taste
- 6 thin slices of crisp apple (Granny Smith or Honeycrisp work great)
- Caramel sauce for drizzling, Optional: pinch of cinnamon or nutmeg

Instructions:

1. **Make the Filling:**
   Slice eggs in half, mash yolks with mayo, mustard, vinegar, salt, and pepper until smooth.
2. **Fill the Eggs:** Spoon or pipe the yolk mixture back into the whites.
3. **Top with Apple & Caramel:**
   Place a thin apple slice on top of each filled egg.
   Drizzle lightly with caramel sauce.
   Optional: add a tiny sprinkle of cinnamon for cozy fall flavor.
4. **Serve for Maximum "What Did I Just Eat?" Energy:**
   Perfect for harvest parties, snack tables, or blowing people's minds at brunch.

Bacon Bit Bonanza

Bacon Bit Bonanza

A deviled egg filled with creamy yellow yolk mixture, piled high with crispy bacon bits

Ingredients:

- 6 hard-boiled eggs, peeled
- 3 tbsp mayonnaise, 1 tsp yellow mustard
- 1/2 tsp vinegar or pickle juice. Salt & pepper, to taste
- 2–3 tbsp crispy bacon bits (or veggie bacon bits)
- Optional: pinch of smoked paprika

Instructions:

1. **Make the Classic Filling:**
   Slice eggs, remove yolks, and mash with mayo, mustard, vinegar, salt, and pepper until creamy.
2. **Pipe & Sprinkle:**
   Fill the egg whites with the yolk mixture.
   Top generously with crispy bacon bits.
3. **Optional Fancy Touch:**
   Add a tiny sprinkle of smoked paprika or chives for color and kick.
4. **Serve Like a Snack Hero:**
   Perfect for brunches, tailgates, and bacon-obsessed snackers.

Banana Slice & Peanut Butter Drizzle

Banana Slice & Peanut Butter Drizzle

The King's Yolk. A little Elvis. A lotta egg. Topped with banan and peanut butter.

Ingredients:

- 6 hard-boiled eggs, peeled
- 3 tbsp mayonnaise, 1 tsp yellow mustard
- 1/2 tsp honey or maple syrup (optional, for sweetness), Salt & pepper, to taste
- 6 thin banana slices (about the size of a nickel)
- Peanut butter (slightly warmed for easy drizzling). Optional: a sprinkle of chopped peanuts or mini bacon crumbles

Instructions:

1. **Make the Filling:**
   Mash yolks with mayo, mustard, honey, salt, and pepper until smooth.
2. **Fill with Flair:** Pipe or spoon the yolk mixture into egg whites.
   Top with a single banana slice.
3. **Drizzle Like a Rockstar:**
   Using a spoon or piping bag, drizzle a thin line of peanut butter over the banana and yolk.
   Optional: sprinkle chopped peanuts or bacon bits for extra Elvis flair.
4. **Serve With Swagger:**
   Perfect for snack tables, brunch, or a hunger-struck Elvis impersonator.

Candy Corn Hat Deviled Egg

Candy Corn Hat Deviled Egg

A deviled egg with creamy yellow yolk filling, topped with a single candy corn placed upright like a tiny festive hat

Ingredients:

- 6 hard-boiled eggs, peeled
- 3 tbsp mayonnaise, 1 tsp yellow mustard
- 1/2 tsp maple syrup or honey (optional for sweetness)
- Salt & pepper, to taste
- 6 candy corn pieces. Optional: a pinch of edible glitter or Halloween sprinkles

Instructions:

1. **Mix It Up:**
   Mash yolks with mayo, mustard, syrup (if using), salt, and pepper until smooth.
2. **Fill the Eggs:** Pipe or spoon the mixture into egg whites.
3. **Crown with Candy Corn:**
   Press a single candy corn gently into the center of each deviled egg, tip up like a little party hat.
   Optional: sprinkle with edible glitter or festive sprinkles.
4. **Serve at Your Own Risk (or Delight):**
   Best for Halloween parties, prank snacks, or candy-loving guests.

Cereal Marshmallows Only (Lucky Charms Style)

Cereal Marshmallows Only (Lucky Charms Style)

Charmageddon. It is Magically confusing. Shockingly tasty.

Ingredients:

- 6 hard-boiled eggs, peeled
- 3 tbsp mayonnaise, 1 tsp yellow mustard
- 1/2 tsp honey or maple syrup (optional for sweetness)
- Salt & pepper, to taste
- 12–18 cereal marshmallows (the colorful kind from Lucky Charms)
- Optional: edible glitter or confetti sprinkles

Instructions:

1. **Mix the Filling:**
   Mash yolks with mayo, mustard, honey, salt, and pepper until smooth.
2. **Pipe & Charm:**
   Fill the egg whites with the yolk mixture.
   Top each with 2–3 colorful cereal marshmallows pressed gently into the yolk.
3. **Optional Sprinkle Party:**
   Add edible glitter or colorful sprinkles for an extra dose of chaos.
4. **Serve with a Side of Whimsy:**
   Ideal for birthday parties, sleepovers, or Saturday morning cartoon marathons.

Chocolate Chip Hat

Chocolate Chip Hat

Chip Happens. Tagline: For dessert rebels only.

Ingredients:

- 6 hard-boiled eggs, peeled
- 3 tbsp mayonnaise. 1 tsp yellow mustard
- 1/2 tsp honey or maple syrup (optional, for sweet vibe)
- Salt & pepper, to taste
- 6 semi-sweet or milk chocolate chips (one per egg)
- Optional: tiny sprinkle of sea salt flakes

Instructions:

1. **Classic Filling with a Sweet Twist:**
   Mash yolks with mayo, mustard, honey, salt, and pepper until smooth.
2. **Fill & Crown:** Spoon or pipe filling into egg whites.
   Place one chocolate chip pointy-side up in the center of each yolk like a little hat.
3. **Optional Finishing Touch:**
   Sprinkle with a flake of sea salt for that sweet-savory hit.
4. **Serve to the Brave & Curious:**
   Perfect for candy lovers, prank snackers, or late-night "why not?" munchies.

Cotton Candy Puff (blue)

Cotton Candy Puff

Egg Cloud 9. Tagline: So sweet, so soft... so confusing.

Ingredients:

- 6 hard-boiled eggs, peeled
- 3 tbsp mayonnaise
- 1 tsp yellow mustard
- 1/2 tsp honey or maple syrup (optional)
- Salt & pepper, to taste
- 6 small tufts of cotton candy (pink, blue, or pastel)

Instructions:

1. **Whip Up the Filling:**
   Mash yolks with mayo, mustard, honey, salt, and pepper until smooth.
2. **Fill & Fluff:**
   Pipe or spoon the yolk mixture into egg whites.
   Right before serving, gently place a small tuft of cotton candy on top of each egg.
3. **Serve Fast & Fabulous:**
   The cotton candy will melt if left too long — so serve these with a flourish and watch the reactions.

Cotton Candy Puff (pink)

Cotton Candy + Pop Rocks

Cotton Candy + Pop Rocks

Melt Down in Yolk Town. Science, sugar, and a slight pop.

Ingredients:

- 6 hard-boiled eggs, peeled
- 3 tbsp mayonnaise
- 1 tsp yellow mustard
- Salt & pepper, to taste
- 6 small tufts of cotton candy (added right before serving)
- Pop Rocks candy (any flavor)

Instructions:

1. **Make the Filling:**
   Mash yolks with mayo, mustard, salt, and pepper until creamy.
2. **Fill & Puff It:**
   Spoon or pipe yolk mixture into egg whites.
   Place a small tuft of cotton candy gently on top.
   Sprinkle Pop Rocks on the cotton candy or around the yolk — but do this **right before serving** for maximum pop.
3. **Serve & Watch the Fun Begin:**
   Perfect for prank snack trays, kids' parties, or anyone who likes snack surprises.

Crushed Froot Loops Confetti

Crushed Froot Loops Confetti

Confetti Confusion. A rainbow fell on your egg. And we allowed it.

Ingredients:

- 6 hard-boiled eggs, peeled
- 3 tbsp mayonnaise
- 1 tsp yellow mustard
- 1/2 tsp honey (optional, for sweetness)
- Salt & pepper, to taste
- 6–8 Froot Loops cereal pieces, crushed lightly

Instructions:

1. **Make the Filling:**
   Mash yolks with mayo, mustard, honey, salt, and pepper until creamy.
2. **Fill & Sprinkle:**
   Spoon or pipe yolk mixture into egg whites.
   Lightly sprinkle crushed Froot Loops cereal over each egg for a burst of color and crunch.
3. **Serve with a Side of "Did I Really Just Eat That?"**
   Because why not. It's a party after all.

Crushed Oreo & Cream Cheese Dot

Crushed Oreo & Cream Cheese Dot

Cookies have entered the chat. **AKA:** *Crushed Oreo & Cream Cheese Dot*

Ingredients:

- 6 hard-boiled eggs, peeled
- 3 tbsp mayonnaise, 1 tsp Dijon mustard
- Salt & pepper, to taste
- 2 crushed Oreo cookies (cream removed if you prefer less sweet)
- 2 tbsp softened cream cheese

Instructions:

1. **Make the Classic Filling:**
   Mash yolks with mayo, mustard, salt, and pepper until smooth.
2. **Fill & Crush:**
   Pipe or spoon yolk mixture into egg whites.
   Sprinkle crushed Oreo crumbs on top of each egg.
3. **Add the Cream Cheese Dot:**
   Using a piping bag or small spoon, add a tiny dot of softened cream cheese on top of the Oreo crumbs.
4. **Serve with a Cookie-Lover's Grin:**
   Because apparently... this is a thing now.

Fruit Loop Halo

Fruit Loop Halo

Breakfast Halo. Cereal. Egg. Destiny.

A deviled egg topped with a single colorful Fruit Loop cereal ring placed neatly on top

Ingredients:

- 6 hard-boiled eggs, peeled
- 3 tbsp mayonnaise. 1 tsp yellow mustard
- 1/2 tsp honey or maple syrup (optional)
- Salt & pepper, to taste
- 6 colorful Fruit Loop cereal rings (one per egg)

Instructions:

1. **Mix the Classic Filling:**
   Mash yolks with mayo, mustard, honey, salt, and pepper until smooth.
2. **Fill & Halo:**
   Spoon or pipe yolk mixture into egg whites.
   Gently place one whole Fruit Loop on top of the filling like a halo.
3. **Optional Flair:**
   Add a second Fruit Loop beside it if you want that extra crunch vibe.
4. **Serve with Saturday Morning Cartoon Energy:**
   Breakfast? Snack? Joke? All of the above.

Graham Cracker & Apple butter Swirl Deviled Egg

Graham Cracker & Apple Butter Swirl Deviled Egg

Yolk Your Sweet Tooth

Ingredients:

- 6 hard-boiled eggs, peeled
- 3 tbsp mayonnaise
- 1 tsp Dijon mustard
- 1/2 tsp apple cider vinegar (optional)
- Salt & pepper, to taste
- 2 graham crackers (crushed into crumbs)
- 3 tbsp apple butter (store-bought or homemade)
- Optional: dash of cinnamon or nutmeg for garnish

Instructions:

1. **Prep the Filling:**
   Slice eggs in half, remove yolks, and mash with mayo, mustard, vinegar, salt, and pepper until smooth.
2. **Pipe & Swirl:**
   Spoon or pipe the yolk mixture into the egg whites.
   Using a toothpick or small spoon, swirl a little apple butter over the yolk filling like a decorative drizzle.

Gummy Bear Hug

Gummy Bear Hug

Bear With Me Sweet. Snuggly. Slightly terrifying.

A deviled egg topped with a colorful gummy bear standing upright in the center.

Ingredients:

- 6 hard-boiled eggs, peeled
- 3 tbsp mayonnaise. 1 tsp yellow mustard
- 1/2 tsp honey (optional)
- Salt & pepper, to taste
- 6 colorful gummy bears (one per egg)

Instructions:

1. **Make the Filling:**
   Mash yolks with mayo, mustard, honey, salt, and pepper until smooth.
2. **Fill & Hug:**
   Spoon or pipe the yolk mixture into egg whites.
   Stand a gummy bear upright in the center of the yolk like it's giving a hug to the egg.
   Optional: add a second gummy bear on the plate nearby for extra cute factor.
3. **Serve with Sweet, Slightly Confused Joy:**
   Best enjoyed by snackers who love candy and deviled eggs in equal measure.

Jelly Bean sparkle Deviled Egg

Jelly Bean Sparkle Deviled Egg

Egg-citing Jelly Jamboree

A deviled egg with creamy yolk filling topped with jelly beans sitting on top.

Ingredients:

- 6 hard-boiled eggs, peeled
- 3 tbsp mayonnaise, 1 tsp yellow mustard
- 1/2 tsp honey or maple syrup (for a sweeter twist)
- Salt & pepper, to taste
- Jelly beans (small ones or chopped larger ones) — 1 or 2 per egg
- Optional: edible glitter or sugar sprinkles

Instructions:

1. **Make the Base:**
   Slice eggs, remove yolks, and mash with mayo, mustard, honey, salt, and pepper until smooth.
2. **Fill & Bedazzle:**
   Spoon or pipe yolk mixture back into egg whites.
   Top each with a colorful jelly bean (or two). For extra sparkle, add edible glitter or a sprinkle of colored sugar.
3. **Serve with Zero Regrets:**
   Sweet, savory, silly — and surprisingly a conversation starter.

Mini Marshmallows & Pop Rocks

Mini Marshmallows & Pop Rocks

Boom Boom Mallow Egg. Handle with care. May explode (your taste buds). ***Mini Marshmallows & Pop Rocks)*** Who says eggs can't party?

A deviled egg topped with a single mini marshmallow and a sprinkle of colorful Pop Rocks candy.

Ingredients:

- 6 hard-boiled eggs, peeled
- 3 tbsp mayonnaise
- 1 tsp yellow mustard
- Salt & pepper, to taste
- 6 mini marshmallows (one per egg)
- Pop Rocks candy (any color or flavor)

Instructions:

1. **Make the Filling:**
   Mash yolks with mayo, mustard, salt, and pepper until creamy.
2. **Fill & Pop:**
   Spoon or pipe the yolk mixture into the egg whites.
   Place one mini marshmallow on top of each filled egg.
   Sprinkle a small pinch of Pop Rocks on the egg **right before serving** (so they don't dissolve).
3. **Serve Quickly & Watch the Reactions:**
   Pop Rocks work best when eaten fresh — or you'll lose the snap, crackle, and boom.

Pancake with Syrup Dot

Pancake (Mini) with Syrup Dot

Short Stack Snack. Brunch meets yolk. Nobody's safe.

Ingredients:

- 6 hard-boiled eggs, peeled
- 3 tbsp mayonnaise, 1 tsp yellow mustard
- 1/2 tsp maple syrup (to sweeten the yolk, optional)
- Salt & pepper, to taste
- 6 mini pancakes (use silver dollar pancakes or cut regular ones small)
- Maple syrup for drizzling

Instructions:

1. **Make the Filling:** Mash yolks with mayo, mustard, maple syrup (if using), salt, and pepper until smooth.
2. **Fill & Stack:** Pipe or spoon yolk mixture into egg whites.
Top each with a mini pancake.
3. **Dot with Syrup:** Drizzle or dot a small amount of maple syrup over the pancake. Optional: garnish with a pinch of powdered sugar or a blueberry for brunch flair.
4. **Serve with Full Brunch Attitude:**
Perfect for a breakfast buffet or confusing a pancake purist.

Peanut butter & Banana Chip Duo

Peanut Butter & Banana Chip Duo

A deviled egg topped with a banana chip and a drizzle of peanut butter.

Ingredients:

- 6 hard-boiled eggs, peeled
- 3 tbsp mayonnaise. 1 tsp yellow mustard
- 1/2 tsp honey or maple syrup (optional)
- Salt & pepper, to taste
- 6 banana chips (one per egg)
- Peanut butter (for drizzling)

Instructions:

1. **Mix the Filling:**
   Mash yolks with mayo, mustard, honey, salt, and pepper until creamy.
2. **Fill & Duo It Up:**
   Pipe or spoon yolk mixture into the egg whites.
   Top each with a banana chip pressed slightly into the yolk.
3. **Peanut Butter Finish:**
   Drizzle a small zigzag of peanut butter over the banana chip and yolk.
   Optional: sprinkle with chopped peanuts for crunch.
4. **Serve for Sweet & Salty Perfection:**
   Perfect for brunch spreads, snack boards, or daring peanut butter fans.

Peep-A-Boo, I See You

Candy Hop (Bunny Peeps)

These are great ideas for children's parties, holidays, and gender reveal events.

Sandy Beach Deviled Egg

A little sweet, a little savory — this deviled egg brings the beach vibes with a sprinkle of light brown sugar "sand" on the side.

Ingredients:

- 6 large eggs, hard-boiled, peeled
- 3 tbsp mayonnaise
- 1 tsp Dijon mustard
- 1 tsp honey (for a slight sweet hint)
- 1/4 tsp salt, Pinch of white pepper
- Light brown sugar, for garnish (to resemble sand)
- Optional garnish: Tiny cocktail umbrella or edible flower

Instructions:

1. Slice eggs in half lengthwise. Remove yolks and mash in a bowl.
2. Mix yolks with mayonnaise, Dijon mustard, honey, salt, and white pepper until smooth.
3. Pipe or spoon mixture into egg whites.
4. **Arrange eggs on a platter**. On one side of each egg, sprinkle a tiny mound of light brown sugar to look like sand. Garnish with a cocktail umbrella or edible flower for extra beach vibes.

S’mores Crumble (Graham + Choc + Marshmallow)

S’more Yolk Please. Fireside chaos in a half shell.

Prepare deviled eggs as usual then Garnish.

Top with Crumbs:
Sprinkle crushed graham crackers on top. Add a tiny dash of cinnamon or nutmeg for cozy vibes.

Serve Sweet & Silly:
Perfect for brunch, snack trays, or confusing your relatives.

Sour Patch Kid Sidekick

Sour Patch Kid Sidekick

Sour Shell Shock. First it's sour. Then it's WHAT?!

Ingredients:

- 6 hard-boiled eggs, peeled
- 3 tbsp mayonnaise
- 1 tsp yellow mustard
- 1/2 tsp honey (optional, for a sweet contrast)
- Salt & pepper, to taste
- 6 Sour Patch Kids candies (one per egg)

Instructions:

1. **Mix the Filling:**
   Mash yolks with mayo, mustard, honey, salt, and pepper until smooth.
2. **Fill the Eggs:**
   Spoon or pipe the yolk mixture into the egg whites.
3. **Top with Sour Patch Kid:**
   Press one Sour Patch Kid candy upright into the center of the yolk filling.
   Optional: sprinkle a tiny bit of sanding sugar or sour candy dust for extra zing.
4. **Serve & Watch Faces:**
   Best served with a warning — "First it's sour... then it's confusing."

Sprinkle Me Silly (Rainbow Sprinkles)

Sprinkle Me Silly (Rainbow Sprinkles)

Rainbow Sprinkles Deviled Egg

Ingredients:

- 6 hard-boiled eggs, peeled
- 3 tbsp mayonnaise
- 1 tsp yellow mustard
- 1/2 tsp honey (optional for sweetness)
- Salt & pepper, to taste
- Rainbow sprinkles (jimmies or nonpareils)

Instructions:

1. **Mix the Filling:**
   Mash yolks with mayo, mustard, honey, salt, and pepper until smooth.
2. **Fill & Sprinkle:**
   Spoon or pipe the yolk mixture into egg whites.
   Generously sprinkle rainbow sprinkles over the yolk filling.
   Optional: add a dash of edible glitter for extra silly sparkle.
3. **Serve with Full Party Energy:**
   Perfect for birthdays, snack tables, or just confusing your family.

Teddy Graham + Sprinkle

Teddy Graham + Sprinkle

Beary Delicious. He's not just a snack—he's a mood.

Ingredients:

- 6 hard-boiled eggs, peeled
- 3 tbsp mayonnaise
- 1 tsp yellow mustard
- 1/2 tsp honey or maple syrup (optional for sweetness)
- Salt & pepper, to taste
- 6 Teddy Grahams (any flavor)
- Rainbow sprinkles or colored sugar

Instructions:

1. **Make the Filling:**
   Mash yolks with mayo, mustard, honey, salt, and pepper until smooth.
2. **Fill & Bear It:**
   Spoon or pipe yolk mixture into egg whites.
   Gently press one Teddy Graham upright into each yolk-filled egg.
   Sprinkle a pinch of rainbow sprinkles around the bear.
3. **Serve at Snack Time or Silly Parties:**
   Works best when nobody is expecting it.

Waffle (Mini Deviled Egg

Waffle (Mini) Deviled Egg

Brunchzilla Deviled Egg. AKA: *Mini Waffle + Syrup Drip*

Ingredients:

- 6 hard-boiled eggs, peeled
- 3 tbsp mayonnaise. 1 tsp yellow mustard
- 1/2 tsp maple syrup (optional, for sweetness). Salt & pepper, to taste
- 6 mini waffles (toasted and cooled) — use frozen minis or cut regular waffles
- Maple syrup for drizzling

Instructions:

1. **Make the Filling:** Mash yolks with mayo, mustard, maple syrup (if using), salt, and pepper until smooth.
2. **Fill & Waffle It Up:**
   Pipe or spoon yolk mixture into egg whites.
   Top each with a mini waffle square or round.
3. **Syrup Drizzle:**
   Drizzle a small amount of maple syrup over the waffle and yolk.
   Optional: sprinkle with powdered sugar for brunchy flair.
4. **Serve for Maximum Brunch Chaos:**
   Perfect for breakfast buffets or snack boards that break all the rules.

CRUNCHY (& RIDICULOUS). Party Eggs with Award Winning Chaos

Crunch is king! Chips, cereal, and crispy things rule here.

Crunch Lords & Snack Queens this may be your section. Texture matters. These eggs have it. From chips to cereal, pretzels to tater tots, these toppers were made for those who like their deviled eggs with a little snap, a lot of crackle, and maybe a dangerous amount of crunch.

Mini Bagel Chip & Cream Cheese Dot

Mini Bagel Chip & Cream Cheese Dot

Ingredients:

- 6 hard-boiled eggs, peeled
- 3 tbsp mayonnaise. 1 tsp Dijon mustard
- 1/2 tsp everything bagel seasoning (optional)
- Salt & pepper, to taste
- 6 mini bagel chips (or broken regular ones)
- 2 tbsp softened cream cheese

Instructions:

1. **Mix the Filling:**
   Mash yolks with mayo, mustard, everything seasoning (if using), salt, and pepper until creamy.
2. **Fill & Top:**
   Pipe or spoon yolk mixture into egg whites.
   Gently press one mini bagel chip into the yolk.
   Add a tiny dollop of cream cheese on top of the chip.
3. **Optional Extra**:
   Sprinkle a pinch more everything bagel seasoning over the top for deli flair.
4. **Serve Like the Brunch Legend You Are:**
   Perfect for brunch boards, bagel bars, or shocking your friends.

BBQ Potato Chip Crunch

BBQ Potato Chip Crunch

BBQ Bae-by. Smoky, salty, snackable chaos.

Ingredients:

- 6 hard-boiled eggs, peeled
- 3 tbsp mayonnaise. 1 tsp yellow mustard
- 1/2 tsp BBQ sauce (optional, for smoky flavor)
- Salt & pepper, to taste
- Crushed BBQ-flavored potato chips (about 1/4 cup)

Instructions:

1. **Make the Filling**:
   Mash yolks with mayo, mustard, BBQ sauce (if using), salt, and pepper until smooth.

2. **Fill & Crunch:**
   Spoon or pipe yolk mixture into egg whites.
   Top generously with crushed BBQ potato chips.

3. **Optional Garnish:**
   Add a tiny extra drizzle of BBQ sauce or a sprinkle of smoked paprika for extra smoky vibes.

4. **Serve at Your Own BBQ Risk:**
   Perfect for snack tables, picnics, or bringing serious backyard energy to brunch.

Cool Ranch Doritos Crumble

Cool Ranch Doritos Crumble

Cool Ranch Chaos

Ingredients:

- 6 hard-boiled eggs, peeled
- 3 tbsp mayonnaise
- 1 tsp yellow mustard
- 1/2 tsp ranch seasoning (optional)
- Salt & pepper, to taste
- Crushed Cool Ranch Doritos (about 1/4 cup)

Instructions:

1. **Make the Filling:**
   Mash yolks with mayo, mustard, ranch seasoning (if using), salt, and pepper until smooth.
2. **Fill & Crumble:**
   Spoon or pipe the yolk mixture into egg whites.
   Generously sprinkle crushed Cool Ranch Doritos over the top.
3. **Optional Power Move:**
   Add a tiny extra sprinkle of ranch powder or a micro-drizzle of ranch dressing for max flavor.
4. **Serve with Confidence (and Napkins):**
   Perfect for snack tables, game nights, or straight-up Doritos lovers.

Mini Crouton & Caesar Sprinkle

Mini Crouton & Caesar Sprinkle

Caesar Deviled Egg. A deviled egg topped with a mini crouton placed on the creamy yolk filling and sprinkled lightly with parmesan cheese.

Ingredients:

- 6 hard-boiled eggs, peeled
- 3 tbsp mayonnaise, 1 tsp Dijon mustard
- 1 tsp Caesar dressing (or a squeeze of lemon juice)
- Salt & pepper, to taste
- 6 mini croutons (or cut regular croutons small)
- Optional: pinch of parmesan or cracked pepper

Instructions:

1. **Mix the Filling:**
   Mash yolks with mayo, mustard, Caesar dressing, salt, and pepper until smooth.
2. **Fill & Crunch:**
   Spoon or pipe yolk mixture into egg whites.
   Top each with a mini crouton pressed gently into the yolk.
3. **Optional Fancy Move:**
   Sprinkle with grated parmesan or a crack of fresh black pepper.
4. **Serve Like a Caesar Snack King:**
   Perfect for brunch boards, salad-inspired snack tables, or shocking Caesar salad lovers.

Crushed Cheese Puffs & Pickle Dust

Crushed Cheese Puffs & Pickle Dust

Puff Daddy Deviled Egg. A deviled egg topped with crushed cheese puffs and a sprinkle of finely chopped pickles or dried pickle seasoning

Ingredients:

- 6 hard-boiled eggs, peeled
- 3 tbsp mayonnaise. 1 tsp yellow mustard
- 1/2 tsp pickle juice (for tang)
- Salt & pepper, to taste
- 1/4 cup crushed cheese puffs (Cheetos or similar)
- 1 tbsp finely chopped dill pickles or dried pickle seasoning

Instructions:

1. **Mix the Filling:**
   Mash yolks with mayo, mustard, pickle juice, salt, and pepper until smooth.
2. **Fill & Crunch:**
   Spoon or pipe the yolk mixture into egg whites.
   Top each with a generous sprinkle of crushed cheese puffs.
   Lightly dust with chopped pickles or dried pickle seasoning.
3. **Optional Flavor Bomb:**
   Add a few extra cheese puff crumbs or a dill pickle chip on the side.
4. **Serve at Maximum Snack Strength:**
   Perfect for snack boards, parties, or extreme snackers.

Crushed Doritos & Salsa Dot

Crushed Doritos & Salsa Dot

Nacho Average Egg. This yolk's got flavor.

Ingredients:

- 6 hard-boiled eggs, peeled
- 3 tbsp mayonnaise. 1 tsp yellow mustard
- 1/2 tsp hot sauce or taco seasoning (optional)
- Salt & pepper, to taste. 1/4 cup crushed nacho cheese Doritos
- Salsa for topping (chunky or smooth — your choice)

Instructions:

1. **Mix the Filling:**
   Mash yolks with mayo, mustard, hot sauce (if using), salt, and pepper until smooth.
2. **Fill & Top:**
   Spoon or pipe yolk mixture into egg whites.
   Sprinkle crushed Doritos over each filled egg.
   Add a tiny dot of salsa right in the center on top of the chips.
3. **Optional Extra:**
   Garnish with a pinch of shredded cheese or chopped cilantro if you're feeling festive.
4. **Serve at Full Nacho Power:**
   Perfect for taco nights, game day, or anytime your snack brain says, "Why not?"

Pretzel Stick Wand

Pretzel Stick Wand

A deviled egg with a creamy yolk center and one short pretzel stick poked upright

Ingredients:

- 6 hard-boiled eggs, peeled
- 3 tbsp mayonnaise
- 1 tsp yellow mustard
- Salt & pepper, to taste
- 6 thin pretzel sticks (cut to size if needed)
- Optional: edible glitter or poppy seeds for "magic dust"

Instructions:

1. **Make the Filling:**
   Mash yolks with mayo, mustard, salt, and pepper until creamy.
2. **Fill & Wand It Up:**
   Pipe or spoon the yolk mixture into egg whites.
   Stick a pretzel stick upright into each yolk-filled egg like a tiny wand.
3. **Optional Sparkle:**
   Sprinkle lightly with edible glitter, poppy seeds, or sesame seeds for a magical touch.
4. **Serve Like a Snack Sorcerer:**
   Perfect for party trays, kid's parties, or pulling a snack out of thin air.

Flamin' Hot Cheetos Crumble

Flamin' Hot Cheetos Crumble

Cheeto Dust & Danger. Warning: May require milk and a fan.

Ingredients:

- 6 hard-boiled eggs, peeled
- 3 tbsp mayonnaise
- 1 tsp yellow mustard
- 1/2 tsp hot sauce (optional, for extra heat)
- Salt & pepper, to taste
- 1/4 cup crushed Flamin' Hot Cheetos
- Optional: whole Cheeto stick for garnish

Instructions:

1. **Make the Filling:**
   Mash yolks with mayo, mustard, hot sauce, salt, and pepper until creamy.
2. **Fill & Dust:**
   Spoon or pipe the yolk mixture into egg whites.
   Sprinkle generously with crushed Flamin' Hot Cheetos.
   Optional: stand a whole Cheeto stick upright in the yolk for extra crunch and flair.
3. **Serve Like a Snack Rebel:**
   Best for snack parties, dares, or proving your spice tolerance.

Mini French Fry & Ketchup Dot

Mini French Fry & Ketchup Dot

Fries Before Guys Deviled Egg

AKA: *Mini French Fry & Ketchup Dot*

Ingredients:

- 6 hard-boiled eggs, peeled
- 3 tbsp mayonnaise
- 1 tsp yellow mustard
- Salt & pepper, to taste
- 6 thin crispy French fries (or use frozen shoestring fries)
- Ketchup for dotting

Instructions:

1. **Mix the Filling:**
   Mash yolks with mayo, mustard, salt, and pepper until creamy.
2. **Fill & Fry It Up:**
   Spoon or pipe yolk mixture into egg whites.
   Gently press a single crispy French fry upright or at an angle into each yolk.
3. **Ketchup Dot:**
   Add a small dot of ketchup right on the yolk or fry for that classic combo.
4. **Serve with a Side of Sass:**
   Perfect for snack platters, brunch, or salty snack lovers.

Frosted Flake Crown

Frosted Flake Crown

They're Eggggcellent!. Tony would be proud. Confused, but proud.

Ingredients:

- 6 hard-boiled eggs, peeled
- 3 tbsp mayonnaise
- 1 tsp yellow mustard
- 1/2 tsp honey or maple syrup (optional)
- Salt & pepper, to taste
- 12 Frosted Flakes cereal pieces (2 per egg for a "crown")

Instructions:

1. **Mix the Filling:**
   Mash yolks with mayo, mustard, honey, salt, and pepper until smooth.
2. **Fill & Crown:**
   Pipe or spoon yolk mixture into egg whites.
   Gently press 2 Frosted Flakes into the yolk at a slight angle like a crown.
   Optional: sprinkle a bit of powdered sugar for extra cereal magic.
3. **Serve with a Roar:**
   Perfect for brunch buffets, breakfast-for-dinner parties, or just shocking your cereal friends.

Fruit Snack Frenzy

Fruit Snack Frenzy

A deviled egg topped with a colorful fruit snack (like a gummy-style berry or fruit

Ingredients:

- 6 hard-boiled eggs, peeled
- 3 tbsp mayonnaise
- 1 tsp yellow mustard
- 1/2 tsp honey or maple syrup (optional)
- Salt & pepper, to taste
- 6 small soft fruit snacks (gummy-style) — one per egg

Instructions:

1. **Mix the Filling:**
   Mash yolks with mayo, mustard, honey, salt, and pepper until smooth.
2. **Fill & Fruit It Up:**
   Spoon or pipe yolk mixture into egg whites.
   Place one colorful fruit snack gently on top of each yolk filling.
   Optional: add a couple of mini fruit snack pieces around the egg for extra flair.
3. **Serve with Zero Shame:**
   Perfect for kids' parties, snack boards, or anyone who appreciates a good lunchtime throwback.

Funyon Onion Ring Loop

Funyon Onion Ring Loop

The Ring Yolked Twice. Crispy. Crunchy. Committed.

Ingredients:

- 6 hard-boiled eggs, peeled
- 3 tbsp mayonnaise
- 1 tsp yellow mustard
- Salt & pepper, to taste
- 6 Funyuns (or mini onion rings) — one per egg
- Optional: sprinkle of smoked paprika or onion powder

Instructions:

1. **Mix the Filling:**
   Mash yolks with mayo, mustard, salt, and pepper until creamy.
2. **Fill & Loop:**
   Spoon or pipe the yolk mixture into egg whites.
   Gently place one Funyun on top of each egg like a crispy loop crown.
3. **Optional Sprinkle:**
   Add a light dusting of smoked paprika or onion powder for extra snacky flair.
4. **Serve with Snack-Lover Swagger:**
   Perfect for parties, game nights, or snack-themed brunches.

Potato Sticks “Bird’s Nest”

Potato Sticks “Bird’s Nest”

Ingredients:

- 6 hard-boiled eggs, peeled
- 3 tbsp mayonnaise
- 1 tsp yellow mustard
- Salt & pepper, to taste
- 1/4 cup crunchy potato sticks (like Pik-Nik or shoestring snack sticks)

Instructions:

1. **Make the Filling:**
   Mash yolks with mayo, mustard, salt, and pepper until smooth.
2. **Fill & Nest:**
   Spoon or pipe the yolk mixture into egg whites.
   Gently arrange a small handful of potato sticks on top like a bird’s nest — loose and messy is perfect.
3. **Optional Garnish:**
   Place a single small round candy or edible pearl in the center like a “nest egg” if you want that extra silly touch.
4. **Serve with Snacktime Style:**
   Great for party trays, spring brunches, or snack-themed events.

Mini Queso Dip & Tortilla Chip Shard

Mini Queso Dip & Tortilla Chip Shard

Queso Compañero Deviled Egg. creamy yolk mixture blended with queso dip, topped with a crunchy tortilla chip

Ingredients:

- 6 hard-boiled eggs, peeled
- 3 tbsp mayonnaise. 1 tsp yellow mustard
- 1 tbsp queso dip (store-bought or homemade)
- Salt & pepper, to taste
- 6 small tortilla chip shards (broken pieces)

Instructions:

1. **Mix the Filling:**
   Mash yolks with mayo, mustard, queso dip, salt, and pepper until smooth.
2. **Fill & Chip It:**
   Pipe or spoon yolk mixture into egg whites.
   Gently press a tortilla chip shard into the yolk like it's ready for a mini dip.
3. **Optional Garnish:**
   Drizzle a tiny bit of queso dip on top or sprinkle with paprika for extra color.
4. **Serve with Tex-Mex Confidence:**
   Great for taco nights, game day, or snacky brunch boards.

Ranch Seasoning & Cheez-It Hat

Ranch Seasoning & Cheez-It Hat

The Cheeze-It Situation. Crunchy, cheesy, questionably legal.

Ingredients:

- 6 hard-boiled eggs, peeled
- 3 tbsp mayonnaise
- 1 tsp yellow mustard
- 1/2 tsp ranch seasoning mix
- Salt & pepper, to taste
- 6 Cheez-It crackers (one per egg)

Instructions:

1. **Make the Filling:**
   Mash yolks with mayo, mustard, ranch seasoning, salt, and pepper until creamy.

2. **Fill & Top:**
   Pipe or spoon yolk mixture into egg whites.
   Sprinkle a tiny bit of ranch seasoning on top of the yolk.
   Place one Cheez-It cracker gently on top like a jaunty little hat.

3. **Optional Crunch Move:**
   Add a few crushed Cheez-It crumbs around the egg for snacky flair.

4. **Serve with Full Snack Authority:**
   Perfect for party trays, snack boards, or unapologetic cheesy moments.

Crushed Takis Tornado

Crushed Takis Tornado

Deviled & Dangerous. Spice level: teenage dare.

Ingredients:

- 6 hard-boiled eggs, peeled
- 3 tbsp mayonnaise
- 1 tsp yellow mustard
- 1/2 tsp hot sauce (optional)
- Salt & pepper, to taste
- 1/4 cup crushed Takis (Fuego flavor or your fave)
- Optional: lime wedge for garnish

Instructions:

1. **Make the Filling:**
   Mash yolks with mayo, mustard, hot sauce, salt, and pepper until creamy.
2. **Fill & Tornado It:**
   Spoon or pipe yolk mixture into egg whites.
   Top each with a generous sprinkle of crushed Takis.
   Optional: stand a small Takis piece upright in the yolk for dramatic effect.
3. **Serve with Spice Level Warnings:**
   Perfect for snack parties, dare games, or spice fanatics.

OUT THERE (& MAYBE SAVORY)

The real-deal flavor bombs. Great for kids who love lunchables, pizza, or mom's leftovers.

Candy Bacon Crumbles

Candy Bacon Crumbles

Sugar, Spice & Bacon on Ice. Sweet. Savory. Sinful.

Ingredients:

- 6 hard-boiled eggs, peeled
- 3 tbsp mayonnaise. 1 tsp yellow mustard
- 1/2 tsp maple syrup (for sweetness)
- Salt & pepper, to taste
- 1/4 cup candied bacon crumbles (or veggie bacon alternative)

For Candied Bacon:

- 2 slices bacon. 2 tbsp brown sugar

Make Candied Bacon:

1. Coat bacon slices with brown sugar.
2. Bake at 375°F (190°C) for 15–20 mins until crispy.
3. Cool completely, then crumble.

Instructions:

1. **Make the Filling:**
   Mash yolks with mayo, mustard, maple syrup, salt, and pepper until smooth.
2. **Fill & Sprinkle:**
   Spoon or pipe yolk mixture into egg whites.
   Top generously with candied bacon crumbles.
3. **Optional Fancy Finish:**
   Drizzle with a tiny bit of maple syrup for extra sweet-and-savory goodness.
4. **Serve Like a Brunch Rockstar:**
   Perfect for brunch boards, snack trays, or bacon fanatics.

Mini Corn Dog Deviled Egg

Mini Corn Dog Deviled Egg

The Fairground Fiasco. Tastes like a carnival. Without the cleanup.

Ingredients:

- 6 hard-boiled eggs, peeled
- 3 tbsp mayonnaise. 1 tsp yellow mustard
- Salt & pepper, to taste
- 6 mini corn dogs (or cut slices of regular corn dogs)
- Ketchup & mustard for drizzling

Instructions:

1. **Mix the Filling:**
   Mash yolks with mayo, mustard, salt, and pepper until smooth.
2. **Fill & Top:**
   Pipe or spoon yolk mixture into egg whites.
   Place a mini corn dog slice on top of each filled egg.
3. **Drizzle for Drama:**
   Add a small zigzag of ketchup and mustard over the corn dog slice.
   Optional: serve with a tiny skewer or toothpick for that fairground vibe.
4. **Serve with Full Carnival Energy:**
   Perfect for party trays, snack boards, or bringing county fair chaos to brunch.

Cornbread Cube + Hot Sauce

Cornbread Cube + Hot Sauce

Brunchzilla Jr. Deviled Egg

Ingredients:

- 6 hard-boiled eggs, peeled
- 3 tbsp mayonnaise. 1 tsp yellow mustard
- 1 tsp honey or maple syrup (optional, for a touch of sweet)
- Salt & pepper, to taste
- 6 mini cornbread cubes (about 1/2 inch each) — homemade or store-bought
- Hot sauce (your favorite brand)

Instructions:

1. **Mix the Filling:**
   Mash yolks with mayo, mustard, honey (if using), salt, and pepper until smooth.
2. **Fill & Top:**
   Spoon or pipe yolk mixture into egg whites.
   Place one mini cube of cornbread gently on top of the yolk.
3. **Hot Sauce Hit:**
   Drizzle a tiny zigzag or dot of hot sauce over the cornbread cube.
4. **Serve with a Sweet Heat Attitude:**
   Perfect for brunch buffets, snack boards, or anyone who loves a sweet-heat combo.

Falafel & Cucumber Dot

Falafel & Cucumber Dot

Falafel Me, Maybe? Deviled Egg

Ingredients:

- 6 hard-boiled eggs, peeled
- 3 tbsp mayonnaise
- 1 tsp tahini or lemon juice (optional)
- 1/2 tsp ground cumin or za'atar seasoning (optional)
- Salt & pepper, to taste
- 6 mini falafel pieces (or cut falafel balls into small chunks)
- 6 thin cucumber slices or tiny cucumber dots

Instructions:

1. **Make the Filling:**
   Mash yolks with mayo, tahini/lemon juice, cumin, salt, and pepper until smooth.
2. **Fill & Top:**
   Pipe or spoon yolk mixture into egg whites.
   Place a small falafel piece on top of the yolk.
   Garnish with a cucumber dot or thin slice for a fresh finish.
3. **Serve with Snack Table Sophistication:**
   Perfect for mezze platters, brunch boards, or bringing a global twist to your silly egg lineup.

Tiny Ham Cube & Pineapple Silver

Tiny Ham Cube & Pineapple Sliver

Hamma-Lamma-Ding-Yolk. Hawaiian pizza's cousin. We don't talk about it.

Ingredients:

- 6 hard-boiled eggs, peeled
- 3 tbsp mayonnaise. 1 tsp yellow mustard
- 1 tsp pineapple juice (optional, for a tropical kick)
- Salt & pepper, to taste
- 6 small cubes of cooked ham
- 6 thin pineapple slivers (fresh or canned)

Instructions:

1. **Mix the Filling:**
   Mash yolks with mayo, mustard, pineapple juice, salt, and pepper until smooth.
2. **Fill & Top:**
   Spoon or pipe yolk mixture into egg whites.
   Place one ham cube and one pineapple sliver on top of each yolk-filled egg.
3. **Optional Garnish:**
   Add a tiny sprinkle of paprika or chopped parsley for color.
4. **Serve with Full Luau Vibes:**
   Perfect for party trays, tropical brunches, or snack boards that don't take themselves too seriously.

Tiny Meatball & Parmesan Sprinkle

Tiny Meatball & Parmesan Sprinkle

Mama mia, that's-a weird-a.

Ingredients:

- 6 hard-boiled eggs, peeled
- 3 tbsp mayonnaise. 1 tsp Dijon mustard
- 1 tbsp grated parmesan cheese
- Salt & pepper, to taste
- 6 small cooked meatball slices or mini meatballs (store-bought or homemade)
- Optional: marinara sauce drizzle

Instructions:

1. **Make the Filling:**
   Mash yolks with mayo, mustard, parmesan, salt, and pepper until creamy.
2. **Fill & Top:**
   Pipe or spoon yolk mixture into egg whites.
   Place one mini meatball slice on top of the yolk.
   Optional: drizzle lightly with marinara sauce.
3. **Parmesan Finish:**
   Sprinkle a little extra grated parmesan over the top.
4. **Serve with a Big Italian Snack Smile:**
   Great for party trays, Italian-themed nights, or your next silly snack board.

Pepperoni & Mozzarella (Pizza Egg)

Pepperoni & Mozzarella (Pizza Egg)

Pizzegg My Heart. Not delivery. Just deviled.

Ingredients:

- 6 hard-boiled eggs, peeled
- 3 tbsp mayonnaise. 1 tsp yellow mustard
- 1 tbsp shredded mozzarella cheese
- Salt & pepper, to taste
- 6 mini pepperoni slices (or cut regular ones small)
- Optional: Italian seasoning or red pepper flakes

Instructions:

1. **Make the Filling:**
   Mash yolks with mayo, mustard, mozzarella, salt, and pepper until smooth.
2. **Fill & Top:**
   Pipe or spoon yolk mixture into egg whites.
   Place one mini pepperoni slice on top of the yolk.
   Optional: lightly sprinkle with Italian seasoning or red pepper flakes.
3. **Optional Melt Move:**
   Give it a quick broil or torch to melt the cheese slightly (totally optional but epic).
4. **Serve Like the Pizza King You Are:**
   Perfect for snack trays, pizza parties, or shocking Italian food purists.

Mini Pickle Slice

Mini Pickle Slice

Pickle Me This. It's tangy. It's weird. It's wonderful.

Ingredients:

- 6 hard-boiled eggs, peeled
- 3 tbsp mayonnaise
- 1 tsp yellow mustard
- 1 tsp pickle juice
- Salt & pepper, to taste
- 6 thin dill pickle slices (round chips or sandwich slices cut small)

Instructions:

1. **Mix the Filling:**
   Mash yolks with mayo, mustard, pickle juice, salt, and pepper until smooth.
2. **Fill & Pickle It:**
   Spoon or pipe yolk mixture into egg whites.
   Place one thin pickle slice on top of each filled egg.
3. **Optional Sprinkle:**
   Add a dash of dried dill or ranch seasoning for extra tang.
4. **Serve with Zero Regrets:**
   Great for snack trays, party boards, or pickle fanatics everywhere.

Sausage Link Crown

Sausage Link Crown

Sausage Royale. Crown your egg. Rule your brunch.

Ingredients:

- 6 hard-boiled eggs, peeled
- 3 tbsp mayonnaise
- 1 tsp Dijon mustard
- Salt & pepper, to taste
- 6 small slices of cooked breakfast sausage link (or veggie sausage)
- **Optional**: chives or shredded cheese for garnish

Instructions:

1. **Make the Filling:**
   Mash yolks with mayo, mustard, salt, and pepper until smooth.
2. **Fill & Crown:**
   Pipe or spoon yolk mixture into egg whites.
   Place one sausage slice upright or slightly tilted on top like a crown.
   Optional: garnish with a sprinkle of chopped chives or shredded cheese.
3. **Serve with Brunch Royalty Energy:**
   Great for breakfast spreads, snack boards, or anyone who believes brunch is a lifestyle.

Sloppy Joe Slather

Sloppy Joe Slather

Messy, meaty, magnificent.

Ingredients:

- 6 hard-boiled eggs, peeled
- 3 tbsp mayonnaise. 1 tsp yellow mustard
- Salt & pepper, to taste
- 3 tbsp cooked sloppy joe meat (well-drained)
- Optional: shredded cheddar or a sprinkle of chives

Instructions:

1. **Make the Filling:**
   Mash yolks with mayo, mustard, salt, and pepper until smooth.
2. **Fill & Slather:**
   Spoon or pipe yolk mixture into egg whites.
   Top each egg with a small dollop of sloppy joe meat.
3. **Optional Topping:**
   Sprinkle with shredded cheddar or chopped chives for extra flair.
4. **Serve with Napkins (Seriously):**
   Perfect for party snack boards, game day, or feeding your inner comfort food lover.

Taco Shell & Salsa Dot

Taco Shell & Salsa Dot

Eggs Over El Paso Deviled Egg. Yolk mixture blended with taco seasoning, topped with a small dollop of chunky salsa and a crunchy taco shell shard standing upright in the center.

Ingredients:

- 6 hard-boiled eggs, peeled
- 3 tbsp mayonnaise. 1 tsp yellow mustard
- 1/2 tsp taco seasoning. Salt & pepper, to taste
- 1 small crunchy taco shell or tortilla chip, broken into 6 shards
- 2 tbsp thick salsa (mild or spicy — you do you)

Instructions:

1. **Make the Filling**: Mash yolks with mayo, mustard, taco seasoning, salt, and pepper until creamy and blended.
2. **Fill & Fiesta:**
   Pipe or spoon yolk mixture into halved egg whites.
   Top each with a tiny dot of salsa and press a small taco shell shard into the yolk mixture upright like a mini nacho sail.
3. **Optional Garnish**:
   Add a sprinkle of shredded cheese, green onion, or crushed tortilla chip crumbs for extra flair.
4. **Serve With Snackable Southwest Swagger:**
   Perfect for Taco Tuesday, brunch fiestas, or when you want all your snacks in one bite.

String Bean Tempura Swords

String Bean Tempura Swords

Bean There, Fried That Deviled Egg

Ingredients:

- 6 hard-boiled eggs, peeled
- 3 tbsp mayonnaise
- 1 tsp yellow mustard
- Salt & pepper, to taste
- 6 crispy tempura string beans (or air-fried green beans)
- Optional: sesame seeds or soy drizzle for garnish

Instructions:

1. **Make the Filling:**
   Mash yolks with mayo, mustard, salt, and pepper until creamy.
2. **Fill & Sword It Up:**
   Pipe or spoon yolk mixture into egg whites.
   Place one crispy tempura green bean into each yolk-filled egg like a sword.
3. **Optional Flavor Boost:**
   Sprinkle sesame seeds or drizzle a tiny bit of soy sauce over the top.
4. **Serve with Full Snack Warrior Energy:**
   Perfect for party trays, snack boards, or your next brunch battle.

Green Peas (Polka Dots) Deviled Eggs

Green Peas (Green Polka Dots)

Green Polka Dot Party Deviled Egg. *Green Peas (or Edamame) Topping*

Ingredients:

- 6 hard-boiled eggs, peeled
- 3 tbsp mayonnaise. 1 tsp yellow mustard
- Salt & pepper, to taste
- 1/4 cup cooked green peas (or shelled edamame). I like raw crunchy sweet peas. You might try that as an option.
- Optional: drizzle of sesame oil or sprinkle of sea salt

Instructions:

1. **Make the Filling:** Mash yolks with mayo, mustard, salt, and pepper until creamy.
2. **Fill & Dot:** Spoon or pipe yolk mixture into egg whites.
   Place 3–4 green peas or edamame on top of each yolk like little green polka dots.
3. **Optional Flavor Pop:**
   Drizzle lightly with sesame oil or sprinkle sea salt for extra taste.
4. **Serve with Veggie Snack Swagger:**
   Great for veggie platters, brunch boards, or just making your eggs a little extra cute.

Mini Fried Chicken Nugget Chunk *Needs no recipe, just let your imagination lead you!*

TOTALLY WEIRD (but we love them)

These are the wild cards. They make no sense while at the same time, they make ALL the sense.

Oh, there are more totally weird recipes to come. Some need no explanation, while many defy organization. Whether you're trying to get your picky eater to eat, you've got a crazy hankering for something, or you want to impress at a party, this book has got it.

Science can't explain what's happening in this section — and honestly, neither can we. These deviled eggs are combinations nobody asked for, but somehow… they work. Kinda. Maybe. Proceed with laughter (and maybe a napkin).

Gummy Pizza Slice

Gummy Pizza Slice

Little Slice of What?!. s it dinner? Is it candy? Yes.

Ingredients:

- 6 hard-boiled eggs, peeled
- 3 tbsp mayonnaise. 1 tsp yellow mustard
- 1/2 tsp honey or maple syrup (optional)
- Salt & pepper, to taste
- 6 mini gummy pizza slices (candy).
- If you are feeling adventurous, cut a tiny piece of real pizza instead of the gummy pizza candy.

Instructions:

1. **Mix the Filling:**
   Mash yolks with mayo, mustard, honey, salt, and pepper until creamy.
2. **Fill & Slice It:**
   Spoon or pipe yolk mixture into egg whites.
   Place one mini gummy pizza slice right on top of each yolk.
3. **Serve with Full Snack Confusion Energy:**
   Perfect for party trays, snack boards, or daring candy lovers.

Ketchup & Mustard Zigzag

Ketchup & Mustard Zigzag

Hot Dog Energy. The picnic came early... and forgot the bun.

Ingredients:

- 6 hard-boiled eggs, peeled
- 3 tbsp mayonnaise
- 1 tsp yellow mustard (for the filling)
- Salt & pepper, to taste
- Ketchup & mustard (for topping)

Instructions:

1. **Mix the Filling:**
   Mash yolks with mayo, mustard, salt, and pepper until creamy.
2. **Fill & Zigzag:**
   Spoon or pipe yolk mixture into egg whites.
   Drizzle a playful zigzag of ketchup and mustard over the yolk.
   Optional: top with a pickle chip or diced onion for a hot dog stand twist.
3. **Serve Like a Picnic Pro:**
   Perfect for BBQ snack boards, backyard brunches, or pure snack-time mischief.

PB&J Dot Combo

Yolk, Meet Sandwich. Childhood memories, scrambled. No recipe required.

Fee Fi Pho Fum Noodles Nest

Spray Cheese Swirl

Spray Cheese Swirl

Say Cheese, Baby. The most unholy union of dairy and yolk.

Ingredients:

- 6 hard-boiled eggs, peeled
- 3 tbsp mayonnaise
- 1 tsp yellow mustard
- Salt & pepper, to taste
- Canned spray cheese (Cheez Whiz or your favorite brand)

Instructions:

1. **Mix the Filling:**
   Mash yolks with mayo, mustard, salt, and pepper until creamy.
2. **Fill & Swirl:**
   Spoon or pipe yolk mixture into egg whites.
   Top each with a playful swirl of canned spray cheese right on the yolk.
   Optional: sprinkle a little paprika or chives for color.
3. **Serve With Full Snack Energy:**
   Perfect for parties, snack boards, or for anyone who lives dangerously with a can of cheese.

Nutella Me About It Deviled Egg

Nutella Me About It Deviled Egg

Chocolate Hazelnut Swirl

Ingredients:

- 6 hard-boiled eggs, peeled
- 3 tbsp mayonnaise
- 1 tsp yellow mustard
- 1 tsp honey (optional for sweetness)
- Salt & pepper, to taste
- 2 tbsp chocolate hazelnut spread (like Nutella)
- **Optional**: crushed hazelnuts or mini chocolate chips

Instructions:

1. **Make the Filling:**
   Mash yolks with mayo, mustard, honey, salt, and pepper until smooth.
2. **Fill & Swirl**:
   Pipe or spoon yolk mixture into egg whites.
   Drizzle or swirl a small amount of chocolate hazelnut spread on top of the yolk.
   Optional: sprinkle with crushed hazelnuts or a mini chocolate chip.
3. **Serve With Sweet Tooth Swagger:**
   Perfect for party trays, snack boards, or the most daring brunch ever.

Banana & Bacon Remix Deviled Egg

Banana & Bacon Remix Deviled Egg

Ingredients:

- 6 hard-boiled eggs, peeled
- 3 tbsp mayonnaise
- 1 tsp yellow mustard
- 1/2 tsp honey or maple syrup (optional)
- Salt & pepper, to taste
- 6 thin banana slices (one per egg)
- Candied bacon bits or crumbles
- Optional: drizzle of maple syrup or peanut butter

Instructions:

1. **Mix the Filling:**
   Mash yolks with mayo, mustard, honey, salt, and pepper until creamy.
2. **Fill & Fusion It Up:**
   Spoon or pipe yolk mixture into egg whites.
   Top each with a banana slice.
   Sprinkle with candied bacon bits.
3. **Optional Drizzle:** Maple syrup or peanut butter for that full sweet-salty fusion vibe.Perfect for brunch boards, snack parties, or when you wanna confuse and delight guests.

Mini Cheese Ritz Cracker Cap

Mini Cheese Ritz Cracker Cap

Ritz & Yolkster Fancy hat. Trashy heart.

Ingredients:

- 6 hard-boiled eggs, peeled
- 3 tbsp mayonnaise. 1 tsp yellow mustard
- Salt & pepper, to taste
- 6 mini Ritz cheese crackers (or cut regular ones small)

Instructions:

1. **Make the Filling:**
   Mash yolks with mayo, mustard, salt, and pepper until smooth.
2. **Fill & Cap It:**
   Spoon or pipe yolk mixture into egg whites.
   Top each with a mini Ritz cheese cracker placed right on top of the yolk like a crunchy crown.
3. **Optional Garnish:**
   Add a pinch of paprika or a tiny herb leaf for flair.
4. **Serve Like a Snack King/Queen:**
   Perfect for snack boards, brunch buffets, or Ritz lovers everywhere.

Rice Krispies Snap-Crackle-Crunch

Rice Krispies Snap-Crackle-Crunch

Snap, Crackle, Yolk! Breakfast just got weird.

Ingredients:

- 6 hard-boiled eggs, peeled
- 3 tbsp mayonnaise. 1 tsp yellow mustard
- 1/2 tsp honey or maple syrup (optional)
- Salt & pepper, to taste
- 1/4 cup Rice Krispies cereal

Instructions:

1. **Mix the Filling:**
   Mash yolks with mayo, mustard, honey, salt, and pepper until smooth.
2. **Fill & Snap It On:**
   Spoon or pipe yolk mixture into egg whites.
   Sprinkle Rice Krispies cereal over the yolk-filled eggs right before serving to keep that crispy crunch.
3. **Optional Sweet Touch:**
   Add a light dusting of powdered sugar or a drizzle of honey if you want a sweeter snack vibe.
4. **Serve with a Crunch & a Giggle:**
   Perfect for snack boards, brunch parties, or cereal lovers in snack-mode.

Toasted Mini Marshmallow & Chocolate Chip

Toasted Mini Marshmallow & Chocolate Chip

Camp Yolkfire. Tell ghost stories. Eat the weirdest s'more ever.

Ingredients:

- 6 hard-boiled eggs, peeled
- 3 tbsp mayonnaise. 1 tsp yellow mustard
- 1/2 tsp honey or maple syrup (optional)
- Salt & pepper, to taste
- 6 mini marshmallows, toasted
- 6 chocolate chips (semi-sweet or milk)

Instructions:

1. **Make the Filling:**
   Mash yolks with mayo, mustard, honey, salt, and pepper until smooth.
2. **Fill & Toasted Top It:**
   Pipe or spoon yolk mixture into egg whites.
   Place one toasted mini marshmallow on the yolk.
   Add a single chocolate chip beside or on top of the marshmallow.
3. **Serve With Campfire Snack Vibes:**
   Perfect for party trays, sleepovers, or shocking your camping buddies.

Crumbled Cookie Dough Bites

Crumbled Cookie Dough Bites

Yolkie Dough Raw cookie energy. Egg edition.

Ingredients:

- 6 hard-boiled eggs, peeled
- 3 tbsp mayonnaise
- 1 tsp Dijon mustard
- 1/2 tsp honey or maple syrup (optional)
- Salt & pepper, to taste
- 1/4 cup edible cookie dough bites, chopped or crumbled

Instructions:

1. **Mix the Filling:**
   Mash yolks with mayo, mustard, honey, salt, and pepper until creamy.
2. **Fill & Dough It:**
   Spoon or pipe yolk mixture into egg whites.
   Sprinkle chopped or crumbled edible cookie dough bites over the top.
3. **Optional Sweet Sprinkle:**
   Add a light dusting of chocolate shavings or a mini chocolate chip for flair.
4. **Serve With Sweet Snack Swagger:**
   Perfect for party trays, brunch buffets, or confusing your cookie-loving friends.

Tater Tot Top Hat

Tater Tot Top Hat

Sir Tottington. Breakfast royalty with a starchy crown.

Ingredients:

- 6 hard-boiled eggs, peeled
- 3 tbsp mayonnaise. 1 tsp yellow mustard
- Salt & pepper, to taste
- 6 crispy cooked tater tots
- Optional: ketchup or hot sauce drizzle

Instructions:

1. **Make the Filling:**
   Mash yolks with mayo, mustard, salt, and pepper until smooth.
2. **Fill & Top Hat It:**
   Spoon or pipe yolk mixture into egg whites.
   Place a single crispy tater tot on top like a fancy little top hat.
   Optional: add a tiny drizzle of ketchup or hot sauce for flair.
3. **Serve With Classy Brunch Energy:**
   Great for brunch boards, snack trays, or showing off your snack fashion sense.

Fried Mac & Cheese Ball

The Carbmageddon. Mac. Cheese. Fried. Egg. You're welcome.

Hot Tamales Deviled Eggs

Hot Tamales Deviled Eggs

AKA: *Yolk on Fire*

Ingredients:

- 6 hard-boiled eggs, peeled
- 3 tbsp mayonnaise
- 1 tsp yellow mustard
- 1/2 tsp white vinegar or pickle juice
- Salt & pepper, to taste
- 6–12 Hot Tamales cinnamon candies (depending on spice level)
- Optional: cinnamon sugar pinch or red sprinkle for garnish

Instructions:

1. **Slice & Scoop:**
   Cut eggs in half lengthwise and remove yolks into a bowl.
2. **Mash & Mix:**
   Mash yolks with mayo, mustard, vinegar, salt, and pepper. For an extra-silly twist, stir in 1–2 finely chopped Hot Tamales (or candy dust). Warning: it's spicy *and* sweet!
3. **Fill & Top:**
   Spoon or pipe filling back into the egg whites. Top each with a single Hot Tamale candy — upright or tilted like a rocket.
4. **Optional Drama:**
   Dust with a tiny pinch of cinnamon sugar or edible red glitter. Serve immediately and prepare for reactions.

Jalapeno Popper Deviled Egg

Jalapeño Popper Deviled Egg

Spicy, creamy, and dangerously good.

Ingredients:

- 6 hard-boiled eggs
- 3 tbsp mayonnaise
- 2 tbsp softened cream cheese
- 1 tsp minced jalapeño (fresh or pickled)
- 1 tbsp cooked crumbled bacon (or veggie bacon)
- Pinch of garlic powder
- Salt & pepper to taste
- Jalapeño slice for topping

Instructions:
Mash yolks with mayo, cream cheese, jalapeño, bacon, garlic powder, salt, and pepper. Pipe into egg whites and top with a jalapeño purchased popper **Optional:** broil briefly for warm popper effect.

A deviled egg with creamy yolk and cream cheese filling, topped with a jalapeño slice and crispy bacon crumbles. Bright, zesty lighting.

ALTERNATE: JALAPENO POPPER DEVILED EGG

Melt Down in the Middle (Grilled Cheese Deviled Egg)

Melt Down in the Middle (Grilled Cheese Deviled Egg)

A deviled egg topped with a mini square of grilled cheese sandwich.

Ingredients:

- 6 hard-boiled eggs
- 3 tbsp mayo
- 1 tsp mustard
- 1 tbsp shredded cheddar cheese
- Pinch of garlic or onion powder
- 1 small grilled cheese sandwich (cut into mini squares)

Instructions:
Mash yolks with mayo, mustard, cheese, and spices. Fill eggs, then place a small square of grilled cheese sandwich on top. Warm slightly for full melt magic.

Bugged Out (Celery + PB + Raisins- Ants on a Deviled Egg)

Bugged Out (Celery + PB + Raisins – Ants on a Deviled Egg)

Ingredients:

- 6 hard-boiled eggs
- 3 tbsp mayo
- 1 tsp yellow mustard
- Salt to taste
- Thin celery stick
- Peanut butter (for topping)
- 2 raisins per egg

Instructions:
Prepare classic deviled egg mix. Fill eggs, then place a celery slice across the top, smear a little PB on it, and press 2 raisins like "ants" on a log. Childhood flashback guaranteed.

🎨 **DALL·E Prompt:**
A deviled egg topped with a celery stick, a small stripe of peanut butter, and two raisins arranged like ants. Plate it on a lunchbox-style tray with fun doodles or school snack elements in the background. Bright, nostalgic lighting.

Pickle Chip & Ranch Dust Bomb

Pickle Chip & Ranch Dust Bomb

Dill or No Dill? The answer is yes. A deviled egg sprinkled with dry ranch seasoning and topped with a crisp dill pickle chip.

Ingredients:

- 6 hard-boiled eggs
- 3 tbsp mayo
- 1 tsp yellow mustard
- 1 tsp pickle juice
- Sprinkle of dry ranch seasoning
- Dill pickle chip for topping

Instructions:

Mash yolks with mayo, mustard, and pickle juice. Fill eggs and top with a sprinkle of dry ranch mix and a single dill pickle chip. Crunch, tang, drama.

Trail Mix Madness

Trail Mix Madness

Camp Snack Chaos Nature called. It brought snacks. These eggs didn't come to play — they came to crash the dessert table. Sprinkles? Yes. Chocolate? Oh yes. Gummy worms? Absolutely. Whether you're a rebel with a sweet tooth or just trying to confuse your taste buds, these sugary yolk bombs are here to make you say, "Wait, is that legal?"

Camp Snack Chaos *(Trail Mix Madness)*

Ingredients:

- 6 hard-boiled eggs
- 3 tbsp mayo
- 1 tsp yellow mustard
- Pinch of garlic powder
- Crushed trail mix (with or without chocolate)
- Optional: sprinkle of flaky salt

Instructions:
Make classic deviled egg filling. Top each with a spoonful of crushed trail mix — nuts, raisins, pretzels, and maybe one rogue M&M. Adventure-ready.

The Pastabilities Are Endless *(Spaghetti & Meatball Mini-Bite)*

Pastabilities

Spaghetti & Meatball Mini-Bite

The Pastabilities Are Endless. It's-a me… Eggio!

If you are an exceptionally bad cook, place the egg with meatball in a plate of Spaghetti-O's or canned ravioli.

A deviled egg topped with a small fork-twirled spaghetti nest and a mini meatball

Ingredients:

- 6 hard-boiled eggs
- 3 tbsp mayo
- 1 tsp Italian dressing or pesto
- 1 tbsp grated parmesan
- 6 tiny spaghetti nests (cold)
- 6 mini meatball slices

Instructions:

Mix deviled egg base with parmesan and dressing. Top each with a twirl of spaghetti and one meatball slice. Sprinkle more parm for flair.

Loaded Nacho Deviled Egg

Loaded Nacho Egg (Sour Cream, Jalapeño, Cheese, Chips)

Extra Loaded & Emotionally Scrambled. The snack with layers. A deviled egg topped with shredded cheddar, a jalapeño slice, and crushed tortilla chips

Ingredients:

- 6 hard-boiled eggs
- 3 tbsp mayo
- 1 tsp sour cream
- 1 tbsp shredded cheddar
- Jalapeño slices
- Crushed tortilla chips

Instructions:

Mix yolks with mayo, sour cream, and cheese. Fill eggs, top with a jalapeño slice and crushed tortilla chips. It's giving loaded nachos with a breakdown.

Deviled Egg Biscuit Sandwich

Biscuit Business. This is not a drill. This is a sandwich.

No instructions needed; just teeth, *right*?

Thank you for purchasing and enjoying this recipe book.

There are five deviled egg recipe books in this series.

1. **State of the Egg:** ***50 Deviled Egg Recipes from 50 States***.
https://a.co/d/ce3Pmgz

2. **City Eggs:** ***Deviled Eggs for FOODIES/ 60 Deviled Egg Recipes from US Cities***

3. **Global Eggs:** ***Seasoned, Stuffed, Dressed Deviled Egg Recipes from Around the World.*** https://a.co/d/1VHjxIm

4. **Veggie Eggies**: ***Vegetarian Deviled Egg Recipes***, https://a.co/d/dCtizz9 and

5. **Silly Eggs: Deviled Egg Recipes for Kids & Folks Who Can't Cook**
https://a.co/d/cRVTSd0

It has been a pleasure. See you in the next book.

Marlene Miles

Avid Home Cook

www.ingramcontent.com/pod-product-compliance
Lightning Source LLC
LaVergne TN
LVHW081633120826
845149LV00025B/1889

* 9 7 8 1 9 7 1 9 3 3 4 6 7 *